POEMS UNDER THE EVER-CHANGING SKY

LALREMRUATI HRAHSEL

ISBN 979-888606299-1

To the introverts and the extroverts,

the lovelorn and the hopeless romantic hearts,

and to the saddest souls....

Contents

1. Ever-changing Sky — 1
2. My Lifeline — 3
3. On Weaker Days — 4
4. The Creation — 6
5. Silence — 7
6. Tell Me — 8
7. Shameless Heart — 9
8. Thought Of You — 10
9. Once — 11
10. Always In Your Heart — 12
11. Unexpected Shore — 13
12. Miss You Silently — 14
13. Separate Worlds — 15
14. Born A Rebel — 16
15. The Restless Heart — 17
16. Let Her Be — 18
17. Desperately Wicked Heart — 19
18. The Circle Never Ends — 20
19. Judge Me Not — 21
20. Dark Clouds In The Blue Sky — 22
21. Madly In Love — 23
22. So Much The Better — 24
23. Heaven In Your Heartbeat — 25
24. Something I'll Never Learn — 26

Contents

25. How Do I? ... 27

26. Clap On And On ... 28

27. Glasses Of Oblivion ... 29

28. In The Same Boat ... 30

29. Girl In A Purple Dress ... 31

30. Her Naked Soul ... 32

31. Fearless And Free ... 33

32. Favorite Stranger Of Mine ... 34

33. Poor Heart ... 35

34. The Player ... 36

35. Sea Of Complicacy ... 37

36. If I Must Die ... 38

37. If Not More ... 39

38. Somewhere In The Universe ... 40

39. Angels' Way ... 41

40. You And I ... 42

41. Don't Leave Just Yet ... 43

42. When He Walks Out Of My Life ... 44

43. A Walk Towards The Beginning ... 46

44. Queen Of Solitude ... 47

45. So You've Been Told ... 48

46. Do It Anyway ... 49

47. Second Thought ... 50

48. Tough To Be Tough ... 51

Contents

49. Story Of Bravery — 52

50. Nothing At All — 53

51. Goddess For My Weary Soul — 54

52. His Slave — 55

53. All Grown Up Now — 56

54. Adios! Dear Old Me! — 57

55. Six Feet Under — 58

56. Isn't It Beautiful? — 59

57. Me And My Mess — 60

58. Unconditional Love — 61

59. Another Heart That Knows Better — 62

60. Something About You — 64

61. Forget Me Not — 65

62. Sadness And I — 66

63. Haunted House — 67

64. Her Highness — 68

65. Seven Years — 69

66. I'll Meet You There — 70

67. One Last Time — 71

68. S.o.s — 72

69. Dust To Dust — 73

70. Where He Fits In — 74

71. Which Road — 75

72. I'm With You — 76

Contents

73. Little Blue Bird 77

74. The Last Laugh 78

75. Sweetest Wine 79

76. Just Tonight 80

77. I Wish I Had Never Met You 81

78. Still And All 82

79. The Last Love Poem 83

80. That Girl 85

81. Love 87

82. Love At First Sight 88

1. Ever-Changing Sky

Speak not to me of forever, my darling,
Unless you can also say with convictions
that hearts never ever change,
And that love always lasts a lifetime.
Promise me not of the things you don't mean to keep, my darling,
And please promise me not of the things you do mean to keep,
For I know too well that you are as powerless as I am in front of
fate.
Comfort me not for tomorrow, my darling,
For you and I have no clue of what plot twist may come in the
next hour,
We are both just two mere fleeting beings in the miniscule
moment of eternity.
So, against the unpredictability of all things under the ever-
changing sky, my darling,
And our insignificance as a tiny speck of dust in the goings-on of
myriad of galaxies,
Let us at least keep things real;
Just be kind to me for today, my darling,
Make me happy to be alive at this very moment;
Tell me that you love me, my darling,
And say those words like

this is our last moment together on earth....

2. My Lifeline

I chase her like she is the blood and I'm the vampire;
Because I need her like she is the heroin and I'm the junkie.
She is a companion ever since the first time I learned what blue
feels like,
She is a friend ever since the first time I understood the grey
shade of life,
She is a lover ever since the first time my heart experienced the
burning red flame of love.
More beautiful than Queen Vashti even in her darkest mood,
More lovely than Queen Esther even in her simplest form,
She enslaves me like I am Samson and she is my Delilah,
And I obey her like I am Adam and she is my Eve.
Rich is what she makes me feel,
No matter how less maybe the zeroes and figures;
She is my companion, my friend and my lover.
Fearless is what I am because of her,
No matter how many maybe the twists and turns;
She is my companion, my friend and my lover.
She is my lifeline;
She is my cure.
And to the world, she is poetry...

3. On Weaker Days

On weaker days,
When your mind is overactive in creating scenarios
just to frighten you,
When the voices of mean people are louder than the little angel's
voice
inside of you,
When fear wraps its cold hands
around your mortal body,
And the beating of your heart won't be calmed down
by your sincere prayers;
I want you to know that,
It's okay to be that afraid,
It's normal to be that weak,
And it's more than alright to lie on the ground
and let the rest of the world go by without you.
I promise you,
A day will surely come
when the cold grip of fear is weakened
by the hands of time,
A day when you'll enjoy the azure sky and your songs again
like you used to;
As for now,

Breathe, embrace the fear, and believe in tomorrow;
After all,
"If winter comes, can spring be far behind?"

• 5 •

4. The Creation

Temporarily built for the battlefield of the dark and white
angels,
Born to toil painfully on the cursed ground until the very last
breath,
Adorned with a beating heart that is susceptible to hurt,
Aren't our bodies the most hapless creation of all?
We do our utmost to decorate the soul's transient abode,
Numbing the cognizance of the fragility of a house made out of
clay,
We lament the death of our loved ones as we talk about our
tomorrow,
Aren't we the most incredible creation of all?

5. Silence

I wrap my anger in silence,
Silence turns my anger into hatred,
Hatred drives happiness away from me.
I wrap my pain in silence,
Silence turns my pain into bitterness,
Bitterness drives my loved ones away from me.
I wrap my fear in silence,
Silence turns my fear into anxiety,
Anxiety drives peace away from me.
I wrap my inferiority in silence,
Silence turns my inferiority into incapability,
Incapability drives opportunity away from me.
Silence is not always gold,
Silence is vociferous,
Silence is treacherous,
Silence is disastrous.
Silence is my downfall,
Silence is my deadliest foe!

6. Tell Me

So tell me,
How long can you run away from your true self?
How long can you go on painting yourself
to match the colour of others?
How long can you keep living a lie
to match the truth of others?
Tell me,
How long can you stay unhappy?

7. Shameless Heart

Forgive my shameless heart,
For falling for you dauntlessly;
It sees not the plainness of its dwelling house,
It cares not the distance between the sky and the earth;
It has the audacity to command my eyes
to look for you every waking hour,
It has the effrontery to imagine
that one day you'll hold me in your loving arms;
It should know better than to dream about you,
You, who should only dine with the best;
It should know better than to long for you,
You, who is God's favourite creation;
It listens not the screams of the world to give up on you,
It heeds not the laughter of the universe for hopelessly loving you;
Forgive my shameless heart,
For falling foy you dauntlessly....

8. Thought of You

As stress was soaking up my brain
like a drop of water
on the sand of the Sahara,
The sky turned dreary,
My songs lost their melodies,
My existence seemed more useless than that of a dried-up pen;
At that worst feeling of low, the thought of you then swept
through my brain,
At that worst feeling of low, I found myself smiling heartily…

9. Once

One moment worth a lifetime,
one conversation worth years of breathing,
once was all granted;
Destiny with its magic wand called fate loves to twirl us around
in this universe you and I are in.
Dreams are painted in the colors of hope,
they are ever beautiful.
In a parallel universe,
you and I are one dream of dreams on the same canvas.
Keep that dream my darling,
I'll keep the hope forever more.
At least our once was better than decades in both the
universes....

10. Always In Your Heart

Maybe you're all that and I'm all this,
Maybe the only answer to all the questions is 'I don't know',
Maybe you and I don't make sense like $1+1=9$;
Still,
I'd like to believe that we met by God's design,
That we are soulmates and are destined to be together,
And that I'm always always in your heart.
Maybe you're frustrated and I'm worn out,
Maybe you and I are caught in the opposite ends of a long-
complicated maze,
Maybe this little pleasure is not worth this much suffering;
Still,
I'd like to believe that you miss me more than I do,
That no other human seems that cool now since you met me,
And that I'm always always in your heart....

11. Unexpected Shore

Unveiling the mystery you wear as an armor,
Leaping through that third layer of your humor,
I see a soul more beautiful than the clear night sky;
Swimming in the pool of your dry words,
Climbing on that wall you built with swords,
Herein lies a heart purer than the morning dew;
Marvelous being in a cloak, look into my eyes once more,
This wave of life may push you to an unexpected shore,
I pray your soul shines forevermore,
And your heart finds its home....

12. Miss You Silently

For you deserve the sweetest fairy tale,
I'll deny my heart and pretend I believe in tragedies;
So, I'll miss you silently darling,
Tell you about the things I want you to know
only through the moon when the world is asleep;
Hug you tight to feel better after a long bad day
only by closing my eyes and imagining you are here;
Sing you a love song
only in the beat of this silent ink;
And see you again soon, my darling,
only in my dreams....

13. Separate Worlds

Like a beautiful dream I had,
but couldn't quite recall;
Our story faded away,
like we never happened at all;
The only good thing in my life,
the one thing that was never meant for me to keep;
Vaporized into a mist to dissipate like the unheard stories of the
past,
and along gone the person I once was before I met you;
I could never go back to the best days of my life that were spent
with you,
and these new days are never getting better without you;
But then who am I to argue with Heaven?
So, I thank the stars for aligning my path with yours once,
And the moon for the existence of someone wonderful,
And the sun for giving me a ray of hope
that we both will be alright
in our separate worlds…

14. Born A Rebel

Born a rebel by nature,
Nothing ever agrees with her,
Her mind and heart are at constant war;
She can be with you and still be a million miles away,
She can be a million miles away and still be with you.
Hungry for new inspirations,
Thirsty for new experiences,
She never leaves a single stone in her way unturned.
Trouble and mistake are her biggest fans,
They follow her wherever she goes.
Yet, she only smiles when it storms,
Only applauds when it hails.
She won't conform,
No, she won't follow.
She is a rebel by nature,
Her heart beats only for the odd and the thrill!...

15. The Restless Heart

The restless heart needs to find its own amusement,
It wants to play,
It needs some sparks;
Now there's a void that needs to be filled,
Butterflies in the stomach that must be set free.
The body got to obey the heart,
It demands pleasure and pain;
The head says it's wrong,
The heart always wins....

16. Let Her Be

Holding her half empty glass,
She adores the half full moon;
She is the half-burnt pages of an anonymous book,
She is the song that takes more than ten fingers to play the chords
right,
She is the distant blue mountain veiled by the dark grey clouds.
After all,
She is not one to be understood,
She is one to be accepted.
She is one you either let her be
or leave her be….

17. Desperately Wicked Heart

Dices are dangling in the air,

The Potter only observes till He calls it time;

Emotions are at the command of our choices,

Our souls at the mercy of our decisions.

The taste of the forbidden fruit proves to be the worst trade of all!

This conscience is forever at odds with the desire of the

desperately wicked heart....

18. The Circle Never Ends

Feeling so hollow it hurts my chest!
Lost here again in the nothingness of reality,
I want to cry for the reason I cannot even comprehend;
Something inside of me must be burning,
Yet I feel part of me has died;
Tired of the same old faces,
Tired of my own reflection;
What am I here for?
Why am I what I am?
An insatiable heart,
Ever wondering eyes,
And a restless soul.
I'm an alien in my own skin;
Always stuck in the middle,
Cause neither of the opposite roads quench my thirst;
The trying, the realizing, the failing,
Oh, here we go again,
The circle never ends!
But I will try, keep trying,
Change my color as the sphere demands;
Maybe one day I'll find it,
That missing piece of the puzzle of my life....

19. Judge Me Not

Oh! Judge me not for always lying in the dark room
with the darkest records on,
Or for finding the most tragic line
the most comforting of them all.
You see, you notice the light in something dark
only when you're in an even darker place;
So let me drown in my ocean of blues
even if it looks pitch dark for you;
This is just me having fun with thousand invisible knives stuck
in my heart
This is just me entertaining my demons so they don't haunt my
soul...

20. Dark Clouds in The Blue Sky

My demon is to stay!
I've battled so hard to slay it once and for all,
All my wasted efforts led me to the inevitable truth,
That none ever wins a battle against fate.
Maybe the dark clouds in the blue sky are what I need,
To be me and stay the way I'm created to be.
I should end this war I'll never win anyway,
Embrace my darkness,
And let there be peace in this chaotic heart.
A little bit of that, a little bit of this,
No one is ever contented in this world anyway....

21. Madly In Love

The way
the mere mention of your name
sweeps my heart through with bliss,
like a gust of heavenly breeze;
The way
just the sight of your face
makes me act like the way people do,
when the first drops of rain finally fall
after months and months of drought;
The way
your presence alone
dims all my worries and fears,
like I'm in a safe haven,
surrounded by rays of happiness;
The way
all the achievements I've ever made
seem nothing at all,
compared with the wholeness I feel
when your arms are around me;
I think Darling,
I think I'm madly in love with you....

22. So Much The Better

I'm no gold digger,
I've got my own silver,
And I'll be just fine with copper,
If your love for me is deeper than the deepest river;
So my darling,
Even if you're not blessed with treasure,
So much the better;
We can lie under the naked sky and count the stars together.
And on starless nights when monsoon defeats summer,
So much the better;
We can run wild under the rain and laugh with the thunder.
And when we grow too old to enjoy the entertainment offered by
nature,
So much the better;
We'll still have each other to fly around with above the ninth
cloud or higher.
Just remember;
All it takes is a love deeper than the deepest river,
To make me yours forever and ever….

23. Heaven In Your Heartbeat

Like a mistake longs for that second chance
to ease the aching consequence;
Like a sinner longs for the sun to go down
to give in to temptations;
Like a ghost longs for a drop of water
to quench his burning thirst;
These arms long to hold you close
to feel Heaven in your heartbeat....

24. Something I'll Never Learn

If appreciating what I have is something
I'll never learn,
I never want to have you then!
Because, my love,
You're someone who should ceaselessly be adored,
Someone who should only be and always be cherished,
Someone who should forever be admired as the brightest star!
So, my love,
Never will I let my shortcomings devalue God's magnificent art,
Never will I let my selfishness outweigh the beautiful life you
deserve.
Though it won't be easy,
I'll gladly learn how to be content with loving you from a
distance,
If loving you as you should be loved is something
I'll never learn....

25. How Do I?

How do I forget you
when even the word forget
reminds me of you?
How do I move on from you
when I need to hear from you
to convince myself that I don't need you?
How do I stop loving you
when my heart refuses to remember
the agony it went through all because of you?
How do I fall in love again
when my soul keeps searching for someone like you
but there's only one you?

26. Clap On and On

You clap along as the trophy you've bled for is handed
to someone new,
Storm is raging inside, but tears are for the pillow,
you must smile;
You had it harder than most,
You wanted it more than most,
You fought for it fiercer than most,
Well,
at least,
You are the one
that Life has chosen to be;
One who is tougher than most,
One who is stronger than most,
One who is humbler than most,
So clap on and on and on....

27. Glasses of Oblivion

Though it's going to wreck me at dawn tomorrow,
Pour me more glasses of that oblivion,
Need to numb these senses that love to torture me.
Reality can't stop being absurd, so why must I stay sane?
Frustration has pushed past what I could possibly endure by 6
degrees,
So can it be so wrong to lessen it by the only way I know how?
Maybe,
Hopefully,
Tomorrow, a miracle will happen and things will get better;
Maybe,
Tomorrow, I'll be brave enough to face things as they are;
But at this aching moment of being stuck in a situation,
that proves to be stronger than
the strength I've been given,
Pour me more glasses of that oblivion,
Need to numb these senses that love to torture me....

28. In The Same Boat

Stitching our hideousness and hope together
as beautifully as we could,
We toil, we fight, we sin today
for the unpromised tomorrow;
Millions of dreams have been achieved,
Millions of dreams have been shattered,
Yet, the happiest ones amongst us
still cry their cries;
Different colors, different opportunities, different beliefs,
Each created nothing like the rest since the beginning;
The beauty and the irony of it all,
We are all in the same boat and Death is our helmsman....

29. Girl In A Purple Dress

That girl in a purple dress,
The sight that humbled the beauties in my head;
Her vibe was enough to enliven the dullest room,
Her spark was enough to light up the darkest mood,
Her aura was enough to chase troubles miles and miles away;
Wasn't it a better world when she was around?
Tell me,
Where did she go when the dance was over?
That girl in a purple dress,
The rainbow to my grey existence;
I searched for her everywhere in town,
Checked all the beautiful and crowded places,
All in vain,
She was nowhere to be seen;
That girl in a purple dress,
The mystery that sent me at my wit's end;
There I finally found her in the least expected place!
Through the window I saw her lying in a small dark room,
Looking more radiant than she ever did
making love to solitude....

30. Her Naked Soul

Once you are done looking and start seeing,
Once you are done listening and start hearing,
Once you are done touching and start feeling,
Her naked soul will embrace you
With the beauty of vulnerability.

31. Fearless And Free

Let us not be bothered by their gleaming smile,
Their house of glitters and perfect family portraits,
You and I.
Let us befriend this emptiness,
and never again be afraid of losing our only friend;
Let us make these longings our riches,
and never again be afraid of getting robbed at night;
Let us make this loneliness our lover,
and never again be afraid of it leaving us for someone better.
Let us bask in the glory of not having it all,
Let us be unbothered, fearless and free,
You and I.

32. Favorite Stranger of Mine

Favorite stranger of mine,
Though we only met not so many hours ago,
Between us there's a flow of energy,
Only the ghosts of poets understand!
So come closer to me,
Let us talk about
Things that will make the Cupid think twice,
Things that will keep our Guardian Angels on their toes,
It is our turn to laugh at the gods....

33. Poor Heart

For her mind loves challenges,
battles and all things intriguing;
Her heart suffers the most.
Because what is good enough
to fascinate her mind;
Is always bad enough
to torture her heart,
And each time her mind is satisfied;
Her poor heart is wronged....

34. The Player

Your smile invites me to cross the river
and be with you;
But they are waving red flags at me,
They warn me not to go,
They say that it's too dangerous,
And that so many have died before me
trying to do the same.
I smile at them and take the first step
leading to you;
They don't know
that I wouldn't even be tempted to give it a try,
If it wasn't dangerous....

35. Sea of Complicacy

Insanity keeps you sane,
Thunder calms you down,
Darkness shows you colors,
Impossible tempts you the hardest,
Loneliness comforts you the most;
There you go again diving in the sea of complicacy!
The shore is made of gold,
But you never say "NO" to pearls....

36. If I Must Die

I have long learned my lesson,
That what is not meant to be can never be;
But like a fool here I am again on the battle field,
Waging war against the invincible fate,
Fighting fiercer than I've ever done before.
No!
You can't tell me to back down
No!
You can't tell me to stop.
I won't hear it
I won't ever surrender!
Know that if I must die,
I chose this as my noble cause;
I'd rather lose my eyes, my arms and my life
than
Not be the one he holds in his arms at night....

37. If Not More

My eyes, they do see the imperfections in his appearance,
Yet they admire them just the same, if not more;
My mind, it does know the flaws in his character,
Yet it adores them just the same, if not more;
My heart, it does feel his heart beating for another woman;
Yet it loves him just the same, if not more....

38. Somewhere In The Universe

He stood there by my window
fumbling for kind lies
to tell me,
I watched him from my bed
ready to act like
I believe it;
His eyes were looking away in such a way
I wish I didn't find it so adorable,
His lips were moving in such a way
I wish I didn't find it so irresistible,
The moment was such in a way
I wish I could make it last a bit longer than forever;
Somewhere in the universe he was with me,
alone,
nobody else,
And that was all that ever mattered....

39. Angels' Way

The angels must have favored her more,
They led her to you first,
While I was sweating in the wrong lane,
Looking for you.
We could have been the resurrection
of Romeo and Juliet,
of Chawngmawii and Hrangchhuana,
Feel the turbulence, the harmony, the ecstasy
Love at its worst, love at its best.
But when our wandering souls finally found their home,
She already has you chained on the ring finger;
The angels must have favored her more....

40. You And I

Prisoners of the conscience,
You and I;
Rain on a sunny day,
You and I;
Slightly damaged beneath the whole,
You and I;
Hushed in our yell,
You and I;
Wrong equations to the right answer,
You and I;
Identical pictures painted in different colors,
You and I;
Two different poems written from the same inspiration,
You and I....

41. Don't Leave Just Yet

If you leave me, my love,
Every new day for me
is going to be as dreadful as the day of execution is
for a prisoner living in a death row,
And that every night I'm going to suffer in a burning hell
set ablaze by your memories.
So, though there are plenty of shiny creations who are willing
to serve you better than I do;
Nicest beings who will treat you the way you deserve to be
treated,
I'm selfishly begging you not to be selfish,
Have a little sympathy for this heart of mine
that needs you the way planet Earth needs the sun
to keep life going on;
Have a little mercy for this soul of mine
that needs you the way the moon needs the sun
to be visible and shine.
So, stay, my love, stay with me a while longer,
don't leave just yet....

42. When He Walks Out Of My Life

Quiet! quiet! quiet!
Stop screaming at me, my senses!
Can't you see there's not enough strength in me
to accept
that his heart is no longer mine,
And that someone else
is now dominating
what was once my peaceful realm?
O Rain! Pour! Pour!
O thunder! Rumble! Rumble,
Hide me from the truth that's looming near like the doomsday,
Save me from the catastrophe that's going to send me
to the loveless hell.
Fine then, fine!
If this is the road that the gods want me to travel,
If they are deliberately paying no attention to my pleas
to restore the love he once had in his heart
just for me;
Be quiet, be still, my senses,
Allow me some time,

a time to learn
how to bleed with grace,
So I could at least fake a smile
when he walks out of my life....

43. A Walk Towards The Beginning

When pain no longer felt like a season that comes and goes,
But a thorn in her heart that grows with everything he does,
She realized her worth was more than his plate of suffering.
She collected the broken pieces of herself through the wasted
years,
Said goodbye to the love she kept alive by watering it with her
tears,
And started walking towards the beginning….

44. Queen of Solitude

Light up the fireworks,
And I'll light up my candles;
Pop open the champagne,
And I'll sip on my black tea;
Dance to the beat of expensive laughter,
And I'll sway to the rhythm of raindrops;
Speed away in those shiny wheels,
And I'll let my imagination drive me to places;
Go on and be happy being the King of Goodtime,
I'll be just as happy being the Queen of Solitude....

45. So You've Been Told

When darkness could no longer comfort you,
When solitude starts screaming at you,
When your thoughts are out to kill every happiness in you,
You need some distractions, something darker than darkness
to ease your mind off of the suffocating pain;
Cuts on the flesh, blood dripping on the cold floor,
Vexing that they don't hurt enough like they are supposed to;
Life is, for you, to endure,
It's the harshest truth you've been forced to learn;
Every new dawn,
the coffin seems more and more like the only door out;
Yet somehow, you manage to shut the door again,
By waking yourself sane with that fresh cut on your flesh;
Another day of holding on,
holding on to the pain,
holding on to anything this cruel world could offer,
All because
the next world won't treat you any better
if you force it open,
so you've been told...

46. Do It Anyway

This is it! The time has come!
Palms are getting sweaty,
Heart is pounding faster,
Chills are running through your veins;
The clock ticks,
Doubt is questioning you now,
You are getting more and more uncertain,
Then the alluring exit door whispers in your ears,
"There is always tomorrow"
The moment is terrifying, I know,
It chokes every particle in your body.
Nevertheless, my darling,
Feel that fear,
Let your nerve be wrecked black and blue,
But do it anyway....

47. Second Thought

Oh, second thought!
You and your meticulousness!
You handcuffed my spontaneity,
Convicted my heart,
And imprisoned my words.
Oh, first thought,
You and your foolishness!
How I wish I could set you free....

48. Tough To Be Tough

Curled up on her fragile bed with the broken
pieces of her dreams,
She tries to ease her boiling frustrations with her warm tears;
The answer to her latest prayer is a "NO" again,
nothing new;
Her pain is already too deep to feel a thing anyway,
it's alright;
Hush now, hush! Don't you say a word!
This is not the time to applaud or to console,
Can't you tell she is not one to give up?
Can't you tell she is going to use the pain to sharpen her knife?
She just needs a little time;
A little time to be weak and vulnerable in the quietness,
Warriors know it's tough to be tough....

49. Story of Bravery

Life may have tamed

your confidence;

Life may have shattered

your courage;

Life may have crushed

your strength;

Let not life,

keep your life,

defeated for long.

Let the lion in you roar louder than those voices,

Let your eagle wings fly you past those storms,

Let the story of your bravery begin....

50. Nothing At All

It burns me inside when I hear you
talking about her;
But let my heart be aflame,
If she is the reason of that smile
on your handsome face.
It pierces me inside that I can't hold you
like the way I want to;
But let my heart bleed a river,
as long as I still get to hold you
like the way you need me to.
It's killing me inside that I cannot tell you that
these words are written just for you,
But let my heart die a thousand deaths as your friend
than having to live the rest of my life
as your nothing,
your nothing at all...

51. Goddess For My Weary Soul

She is the goddess for my weary soul;
She doesn't keep count of the number of my sins,
She doesn't measure the weight of my heart,
She prepares an unprejudiced bed for my tainted body to lie on;
She takes down my vibrant cloak of guilt, then covers me
with her sheet of serenity,
She smiles and sings to me, 'Let it be so, let is pass by'.
She is the goddess for my weary soul;
She keeps me safe from the maddening screams of the chaotic
world,
She whispers to me never before heard melodies
like she did to those dead poets,
She shows me the hours and days that are passing us by,
then locks her timeless window,
She smiles and sings to me, 'Let it be so, let it pass by'.
She is the goddess for my weary soul;
She is my refuge, she is my solace, she is my remedy,
Solitude is her humble name,
"Run for your life, the end is near," screams the world,
She smiles and we sing, 'Let it be so, Let it pass by'....

52. His Slave

Cool maybe the breeze,
Soft maybe his words,
Enchanting maybe the moment,
Triple layered that wall of your precious heart;
For once he breaks it through,
You are doomed to be his keen slave,
body and soul....

53. All Grown Up Now

Mamma is holding my hand
as we are crossing the road,
Not the other way around
like we used to do;
I guess I'm all grown up now.
Pappa is asking me questions
as he is leafing through a new book,
Not the other way around
like we used to do;
I guess I'm all grown up now.
Little kids in our old street
do look a lot like my childhood friends,
They are playing the same games
we used to play;
I guess I'm all grown up now.
"Life is too short" sighs the woman living next door
as she combs her once black silver hair,
The line makes sense
more than it ever did;
I guess I'm all grown up now....

54. Adios! Dear Old Me!

Adios! Dear Old Me!
The unfulfilled dreams left forgotten,
The awards gleaming on my mamma's wall;
The wasted feelings buried somewhere,
The memories too sweet to erase;
The madness, the sanity, and the rare in-between moments,
It was everything and more being you;
But we must go in our separate ways now,
For life is too short for us mortals to replay.
So, Goodbye now, Dear Old Me,
I hope you'll always be warm in the heart of some dear ones....

55. Six Feet Under

Six feet under,
White as snow, still as water, calm as dawn,
She lays there for forever;
Never again will she long for rain on a sunny day,
Never again will she be mocked by her merciless mirror,
Never again will her blind heart lead her to misery.
Roses are red,
Lies are beautiful,
She no longer needs them nor you....

56. Isn't It Beautiful?

Isn't it beautiful
that moment your heart starts fluttering for
that someone new?
Pain disappears like it has never happened,
Hope reappears like it has never been daunted;
The old memories fade away like those dreams in the morning,
The lessons learned seem like some Aesop's fables that you've
forgotten,
And the walls, they crumble down like the walls of Jericho;
But not because your heart gets defeated,
But because it is ready to take new chances.
And it doesn't matter how old you are,
You are once again a beginner, a fool in love,
Isn't it beautiful
that moment your heart is falling for that someone new
like it is falling for the very first time?...

57. Me and My Mess

A second chance just to make the situation worse,
A pro at making a mess is all I'll ever be.
I've learned better now than to wish for another shot;
So, my fingers are crossed this time,
that you may be the one,
who couldn't get enough of me and my mess....

58. Unconditional Love

My shoulder may not be strong enough,
but it's willing to carry the weight off of your shoulder
till all of its strength is gone;
My hands may not be big enough,
but they are willing to fight each of your enemies
till there's no energy left in them to throw the last punch;
My heart may not be beautiful enough,
but it promises to beat only for you
till this body draws the very last breath;
So, allow me to shed my tears for the pain you are hiding inside,
Allow me to patch up those wounds the world has inflicted upon
you;
Just remember, do remember and always remember
that
I've got enough love for you to
keep you loved
many a lifetime and more....

59. Another Heart That knows Better

Loving me isn't the easiest thing to do, I know.
I'm warmer that most during
my summer time,
So warm you readily believe that you've finally found
your forever home!
But then in a blink of an eye,
my winter comes;
You watch me turn into the coldest ice,
So cold you know I won't budge
even if you drown under the Arctic Ocean.
It takes a whole lot to stay with me, I know.
Only Heaven knows what brings about the changes in my
seasons,
And how long they may last is the question that no angel could
answer,
Believe me,
I too wish I could run from my own self every damn time.
So, my darling,
If a day comes when you feel that the winter is too harsh and too
long,

Don't hesitate to walk towards where the sun shines;
The tears are mine to shed,
don't look back;
Doubt not even for a second
that you are another heart that knows better,
And keep walking on away from me....

60. Something About You

Something about you that is naïve,
underneath that devious smile;
Something about you that is gentle,
underneath that reckless demeanor;
Something about you that is shy,
underneath those brazen words;
Something about you that is just as gawky,
Underneath those flawless moves;
The things about you that you chose to veil instead,
The things you chose not to be;
Oh, those are the things that made me believe in that
something....

61. Forget Me Not

Forget me not when the sun bows to the coming storm;
and the dark clouds shroud your surroundings.
Forget me not when you find yourself standing on top of a hill;
and the cool wind blows your worries away,
like they are mere assembled jigsaw puzzles made of paper.
Forget me not when you lay your eyes on
a simple poem written with depth;
and your soul finds the wine to quench its thirst.
Forget me not when you stumble upon some blue flowers
blooming blue at the corner;
and forget not of how I, who was made to bloom in blue,
once asked you to forget me not....

62. Sadness and I

The overwhelming sadness is creeping inside of me again
like it owns me,
like I've always been its property;
This sadness,
it comes as it pleases,
never asking if I've got any reason to feel it so.
Sometimes it chimes in out of nowhere
when I'm most happy,
and entices me with that charm of an ex-lover
who had once dimmed the rest of the world
with just one smile.
So, what I do is giving in, embrace it back like we are always
meant to be
And let it consume all of me.
This sadness and I,
we've been together for countless days of cursing at the sun now,
Believe me,
I don't run from nightmares and monsters anymore;
Not because I've gained enough strength to defeat them,
But because I no longer care if they wreck me....

63. Haunted House

Trapped again in the haunted house of my past,
The maddening screams of the ghosts therein
rob me of my sanity;
Peace won't accompany me any longer,
Tranquillity has deserted me;
And the angels weep because I could no longer feel
their comforting arms.
How did I find myself here again? I do not know.
Haven't I left the place or was it just that
the place let me go like a feline letting go of its prey just for sport,
knowing fully well of its power over her? I'll never know.
I've got enough strength but no courage to open the door,
So I lay myself down with the key in my hand,
waiting for the walls to crumble;
Hoping that one day when you visit the ruin with flowers,
You'll at least find the remnants of my soul that had been set free
with these words....

64. Her Highness

Done being pampered and catered by the angels above,
She decides to come down to earth
to play with the emotions of us unworthy earthlings,
She is bored of the celestial world.
Coquettish, eccentric, destructive,
The most enigmatic of them all.
Down here on earth she spreads her wings;
Weeps with the broken hearts,
Dances with the joyous ones,
Quenches the thirst of the loners,
And taunts the ungrateful ones with a careless laugh.
Time to time she is insatiable, she wants more and more,
Chin up, she walks around like a merciless queen,
Destroying whatever stands in her way,
Till the sky begs the sun to kindly bring her back home.
Along she floats up with the chosen souls
that she has collected,
To be pampered and catered by the angels
up in the celestial world.
Again, she leaves us mystified, petrified but never satisfied!
How I wish I was as half wonderful as her highness,
How I wish I was rain....

65. Seven Years

Am I going to let the seven years I've been here longer

stand in my way of loving you?

Never!

Seven years earlier I was created to exist here;

So I will have explored many perilous roads,

so I can protect you better.

Seven years earlier I was created to exist here;

So I will have dined with the wrong hearts,

so I can love you better.

Seven years earlier I was created to exist here;

So life will have crowned me with roses and thorns,

so I can be your queen and slave at the same time.

If I were to let seven years stop me from loving you;

It would be the fear that,

I won't be able to love you seven years longer.

But here I am, there you are.

Seven years deeper river for us to swim in so we see more,

Seven years fresher river for us to bathe in so we stay trendy,

Let us dive in....

66. I'll Meet You There

Too late, my love, you're way too late,
I've already ruined my life
in failed attempts
to erase the memory of you;
Too bad, my love, our love story will have to be put on hold
till we meet again in the next life,
There, I'll forgive you for breaking the heart that loved you to
death,
There, we'll be lovers again,
get married, have kids, and grow old together;
There, we'll love till death do us apart.
There, I'll meet you there....

67. One Last Time

His skin was lined with regret,
His eyes were screaming her name;
He had long lost the count of the sun and the moon,
All he knew was he needed to see her again;
Just one last time he prayed.
It was one another dreadful day,
He was loitering aimlessly with his aimless life,
Recreating moments the way they should have happened;
Then out of the blue there stood in front of him,
The very image of her;
His heart skipped a beat,
Her eyes, her nose, her smile;
But they belonged to a little boy.....

68. S.O.S

Scream, scream, scream, My Soul!
Let that turmoil inside burn out;
You've been lost far too deep in the woods,
Feeding on rotten plums and poisonous nectar,
Forever waiting on a ray of sunlight to guide you home.
The ray of sunshine you've forgotten what it looks like.
So scream, scream, scream my soul,
my dear soul....

69. Dust To Dust

Dust to dust,
Better the dust that travels with the wind,
Than be the person it blows upon;
Maybe someday when the wind is fierce enough,
It shall blow my dust up into the sky,
Travel on sea to sea,
continent to continent,
century to century;
Heartless my dust will be, fearless and free,
Till the books are opened and it reunites with its soul,
To stand before the throne and be judged one last time....

70. Where He Fits In

A little shy, a little insecure,
Undercover to conquer another day;
Keeping everyone close, but never too close,
In the dark he sheds his mask;
Make-believe world is where he fits in,
A lot depressed, a lot suppressed;
He drags his heavy heart with his light feet,
Maybe tomorrow is the day he ends it all;
But today he smiles so that you may be amused....

71. Which Road

It's a sunless road he's been traveling all his life,
Lately,
with every step he takes,
it gets darker;
There is no going back,
it's a one-way road;
Should he continue his journey with his blood-stained feet?
Or should he put an end to the fate that never favors him?
His dejected eyes are staring at me intently
for the answer;
But which road do I point to
when neither leads to the light?

72. I'm With You

When your reality is your worst nightmare,
And dreamland is the only place where you can truly be happy,
But you cannot fall asleep;
When it seems like the whole world is staring at you
with scorn burning in their eyes,
And the person in the mirror loathes you back
as much as you do,
But they are all that you see;
Doubt not once in your heart
that no amount of wrongs could ever outweigh the love I have
for you,
Forget not that I'm with you,
always with you…

73. Little Blue Bird

Little blue bird sitting on a tree,
She watches as the leaves are flying towards the setting sun,
It's fall, things meant to fall will fall;
She isn't begging them to stay,
She isn't putting up a fight against Mother Nature.
Instead, she spreads her wings and flies up in the sky,
Dances with the wind and floats around with the clouds;
For she knows when she comes back,
The sunrise will greet her again with lusciously green new
leaves....

74. The Last Laugh

You aim your dart like words against me,
Like my ugly isn't already enough to make you feel beautiful,
Like my weakness isn't already enough to make you feel powerful;
The dart hits the target,
Your world laughs as I writhe on the ruthless floor;
My anger, my frustrations, my resentment,
finding no exit through my helpless mouth,
stream out in the form of tears through my helpless eyes;
But these tears, don't you confuse them with tears of defeat,
Hear the silent scream of my wounded soul;
By going through another day with this pain that you are
making me suffer,
The pain, if it was your lot,
would drag you down the cold dark grave,
you are adding another scar onto my skin;
Scars are thicker than skin, don't you know that?
The more you hit, the more resilient I become!
And after all, it's a survival-of-the-fittest world we are living in,
Because of my ugly, because of my weakness, and because of you;
Someday I'll survive what shatters you and your world,
Someday you'll see me rise above and beyond your reach,
Someday, I'll be the one having the last laugh....

75. Sweetest Wine

So sweet, so strong,
You were the best wine I've ever tasted;
One sip,
then I was addicted to you;
You ran through all my veins,
Turned my reality into fantasy;
Just one glass of you to start my day,
And ten glasses more or so just to get me through the day;
Blurred, reckless and carefree,
I loved being lost in your haze.
Should have realized the stronger the drink is,
The harder the hangover kicks in;
Should have known after having tasted the sweetest,
The other sweets lost their flavors;
Cause here comes the dawn,
The bottle is empty;
The smell lingers,
But the high is gone;
It's just me now and the memory of you,
Sober but the messiest I've ever been....

76. Just Tonight

Tonight, I'm going to let my guard down,
And miss you as hard as I want to.
Tonight, I'm going to forget that I've moved on from you,
And let the memories of you stream in.
Tonight, I'm going to pretend that our love has never faded,
And might just ring you up.
Tonight! Oh, just tonight I'm going to be that girl I hated,
And be that girl you once loved….

77. I Wish I Had Never Met You

I wish I had never met you;
So I wouldn't be so affected by the sight of you,
just a stranger,
smiling next to someone who looks perfect in all the ways I'm
not.
I wish I had never known you;
So I wouldn't be so aware of how empty life without you is,
and be ignorantly content with the fucked-up life I've been
given.
I wish I had never been with you;
So I wouldn't realize no next person is ever making me feel again
half the bliss I used to feel,
just looking at those eyes of yours staring back at me.
Oh! How I wish I had never met you at all....

78. Still and All

Confetti over your trophy,
Autumn leaves over my head;
You run so as to win,
I stroll so as to feel;
You think I am weak,
I think you're naïve;
They clap for you,
They sigh for me;
Still and all,
I'm as happy as you maybe….

79. The Last Love Poem

Though the love I have for you in my heart will forever flow like
the river
to the end of the world,
Your love for me had burned out with the rain many monsoons
ago;
And when the world doesn't plan on slowing down for the
broken hearts even just for a second,
I can't stay forever frozen in the time where you left me stone
cold,
So, here's my last love poem for you;
I accept it now,
I won't be the one smiling next to you as you tell your future kids
you love them,
At least I was once the one you told the three words to,
So, I'm grateful, eternally grateful.
I accept it now,
Your love is never meant for me to write poems of true love,
At least it gives me poems of pain, pain out of love,
So, I'm grateful, eternally grateful.
I accept it now,
Your wrinkled hands aren't mine to hold when lying on my
deathbed,

At least they once held me with such an intense amount of love,
So, I'm grateful, eternally grateful.
We may meet again in this world, we may not,
Our promises to meet belong to others now, never to one another;
I accept it now.
Just remember that I'm grateful, eternally grateful,
All because of you....

80. That Girl

I run back to her;
The girl that I shunned,
The girl that I was ashamed of,
The girl that I once was.
I pick her up;
The girl that I despised,
The girl that I disowned,
The girl I wished I was anything but not her.
I wrap my arms around her;
Her ugly,
her folly,
her lot in life.
I beg her for forgiveness;
That girl created her own happiness out of whatever was given to
her,
That girl did what she thought was best at the moment,
That girl ventured into the wild and fought her best fight so her
future self
is given what she was deprived of.
This woman knows better now,
She is who she is because she was who she was,
And from now on,

together,
they'll brazenly be who they'll be....

81. LOVE

Love
Love is something like the sun that warms my heart in the dead
of winter,
And leaves me to freeze
just when I lay myself down to bask under it.
Love
Love is something like the breeze that soothes my body on a hot
summer day,
And strikes me like a hurricane to wreck me
just when I take off my cloak to feel it.
Love
Love is something like the invisible wings that transcend my soul
to cloud nine,
And pushes me down to the ground to shatter in pieces
just when I think I can fly.
Love is something for me to adore from afar, never to touch;
Unless I find comfort in the embrace of loneliness.
Love is something for me to muse upon, never to own;
Unless I find comfort in the embrace of pain.
But if there's one thing I know, I'm certain of this,
If love comes around next time as a poison poured in my cup,
Love is something I'll drink to the very last drop.....

82. Love At First Sight

Haven't the gods had enough laugh
making fun out of my luckless heart?
Or do the angels think it's about time
I believe in love at first sight?
Ever since you walked past me that evening
with a face so gorgeous
my bedazzled eyes couldn't help but chase after you
like you were the setting golden sun,
Yes, since then, you've been stuck in my head
like the melody of a captivating song once heard,
And my heart misses you
like it has lost someone it knows for a long long time.
Could it be that we shared a tragic love story
in our previous lives
that just one sight of you makes me this lovesick?
Or could it be that you are the one for me
like those people in love talk about?
O! that sweet melodious song!
How I would pay everything the universe charges
to hear it again just one more time!
Because here my forlorn heart lies under the sunless sky
feeling like it's never going to feel whole again

until I see that face of yours again,
The face that feels like the missing piece of the puzzle of my life...

Thank You.

Yours,

remihrahsel@gmail.com